ILLINOIS
in words and pictures

BY DENNIS B. FRADIN

ILLUSTRATIONS BY ROBERT ULM

 CHILDRENS PRESS, CHICAGO

Library of Congress Cataloging in Publication Data

Fradin, Dennis.
  Illinois, in words and pictures.

  SUMMARY: A simple history of Illinois with a
description of Chicago's points of interest and
some historical sights of the state.
  1. Illinois—History—Juvenile literature.
|1. Illinois—History| I. Ulm, Robert. II.
Title.
F541.3.F7   977.3   76-7389
ISBN 0-516-03911-3

Picture Acknowledgements:
ILLINOIS DIVISION OF TOURISM—DEPT. OF BUSINESS AND ECONOMIC
DEVELOPMENT—pages 26, 27, 31, 32 (right, top and bottom), 36, 39 (top), 42
CHICAGO CONVENTION AND TOURISM BUREAU—pages 5, 18 (top), 41
A.W. MUELLER COLLECTION—pages 2, 39 (bottom)
INTERNATIONAL HARVESTER—page 28
UNITED AIRLINES—pages 18 (bottom), 25, 32 (bottom left and right)
SANTA FE RAILWAY—pages 4, 16, and front cover
JOHN G. SHEDD AQUARIUM—page 23
BOB ROCK PHOTOGRAPHY—pages 15, 22, 25 (left)

From the air, Illinois (ill • ih • NOY) is a wonderland of color. You see yellow fields of grain, green fields of corn, and winding blue rivers. Hundreds of small towns dot the countryside. There are some hills in Illinois. But much of the land is flat grassland. That is why Illinois is called "The Prairie State."

Aerial view of Chicago skyline

Your plane is landing in Chicago. Chicago is one of the giant cities of the world. Its tall buildings seem to reach up under the wings of your airplane.

O'Hare airport

What a big airport! It is called O'Hare. Thirty-six million people fly in and out of O'Hare each year. Day and night, airplanes come and go. It is the world's busiest airport.

Think about the history of Illinois as your plane lands.

Millions of years ago there were no people here. There was no state called Illinois. There was only the land. And for many millions of years the land was covered by water.

When the water left, the ice came. During the Ice Age most of the land was buried under huge patches of ice called glaciers (GLAY • shers).

The glaciers melted. A layer of rich, black dirt was left. This dirt is good for growing things. That is why Illinois is sometimes called "the Garden Spot of the Nation."

Little is known about the first people who made
their homes on this land. We do know they built
thousands of large piles of earth, called mounds. So
they are called Mound Builders. Bones and pottery
have been found inside these mounds.

Much later many Indian tribes lived on this land. Six
of the tribes called themselves the Illini (ih • LYE • nye),
or "the men."

Explorers Marquette (mar • KETT) and Joliet
(JOE • lee • ett) are thought to be the first outsiders in
the land of the Illini. They came in 1673. They met
many friendly Indians.

Soon others came to live on the land. People from France (FRANSS) settled and grew many crops. An explorer named La Salle (la • SAL) traded with the Indians.

Later on people from England (ING • land) came to live here. Then England fought France for the land. England won this war. Now England ruled all the people—the English, the French, and the Indians.

The land was at peace. More settlers came. But trouble was coming. More and more people in America (ah • MAIR • ih • ka) did not like what England told them to do. They wanted to rule themselves.

In 1776 war broke out between the people in America and the rulers in England. This war was called the Revolutionary War (rev • oh • LOO • shun • airy   wore).

During this war a fighter named George Rogers Clark led a band of men against the English. These men were called the "Long Knives," because of the knives they carried. In 1778 the Long Knives took the English fort at Kaskaskia (kas • KASS • key • ah).

13 New States

Northwest Territory

The Revolutionary War ended in 1783. The English gave up. The land became part of a new country—The United States of America. There still was no state of Illinois. In 1787 all this land was part of the Northwest Territory.

Illinois (red) ranks 24th. in size
among all the States and 8th in size
among the Midwestern States (yellow)

There were many wars between the Indians and the settlers in the territory. In 1812 the Indians killed many settlers at Fort Dearborn (DEER • bohrn) in what is now Chicago (shi • KAW • go). But soon nearly all the Indians were driven from the land.

In 1818 Illinois became the 21st state. About 40,000 people lived there. Five states touch some part of Illinois. They are: Indiana, Kentucky, Missouri, Iowa, and Wisconsin. Illinois is nearly 400 miles from north to south. At its widest place, the state is about 200 miles from east to west.

Your plane has landed. You are in Chicago, a good place to begin a trip through Illinois.

From the ground, Chicago's buildings seem so tall. The first steel skyscrapers were built here. Can you see the Sears Tower? It is 110 stories high.

View of Sears Tower

In 1779 a trader named Du Sable (doo •SAA •bill)
built the first house in a place the Indians called
Checagou. For a long time, this was just a small
village where fur traders met.

By 1837 this was a city known as Chicago. About
4000 people lived there at the time. Today, it is the
biggest city in Illinois.

Downtown is a very busy place. Chicagoans call this area "The Loop" because it is circled by train tracks.

There are people of all races in Chicago. In the early 1900's people came to Chicago from many different countries. They came to work in the city's thousands of factories.

The Loop

Chicago has a strange post office. A tunnel on the expressway cuts right through the main post office. More than 26,000 people work here. That's more people than live in many towns!

Even the Chicago River is different. It flows backwards. Much sewage is dumped into the Chicago River. But people didn't want it to go into Lake Michigan. So, in 1900, the river was dug out. Now the river flows away from Lake Michigan.

The city is right next to Lake Michigan. Can you see the boats in the harbor? There are many fishing boats. Perch, bass, trout, pike, catfish, carp, Coho salmon, and smelt are caught in the lake.

Top: Chicago River
Bottom left: Belmont Harbor in Chicago
Bottom right: Chicago's Lake Shore Drive

Chicago has been called the "Crossroads of America." It is near the center of the United States. More trains go through Chicago than any other city. Farmers send their goods to Chicago. From here the food is sent all over the country.

It is amazing that Chicago is so big. In 1871, most of the city burned to the ground. People had to go into the lake to save their lives. Even in the water people's hair burned from the great heat.

Some say the fire started when Mrs. O'Leary's cow kicked over a lantern. But no one knows for sure.

The Water Tower

The old Water Tower is one of the few buildings that didn't burn down. The people who built the new Chicago left it standing. It reminds everyone of the old days.

Chicago has many places that are the biggest and the largest.

Left: Diver holding fish in coral reef of Shedd Aquarium
Top right: Exterior view of Shedd Aquarium
Bottom right: Coral reef in Shedd Aquarium

The Shedd Aquarium (a • KWAR • ee • um) is the largest in the world. The aquarium is next to Lake Michigan, but it has many more kinds of fish than the lake.

Nearby is the planetarium (plan • ih • TAIR • ee • um). Here you can look at the stars. It seems as if you can almost touch them. And you almost can! A machine shows them on the ceiling.

At the Field Museum of Natural History you can see models of cavemen. There is also a skeleton of a dinosaur and mummies that are thousands of years old.

If you want to learn about science, stop at the Museum of Science and Industry. There, you can go down into a coal mine. It looks just like the real coal mines in southern Illinois. You can also walk through a real submarine. Or see the Apollo 8 spacecraft that circled the moon.

The Baha'i Temple

The Museum of Science and Industry

There are no cities nearly as big as Chicago in the rest of Illinois. But the state is certainly beautiful.

In Wilmette (WILL • met) there is a famous place called Baha'i Temple (bah • HI   TEM • pil). This is the North American headquarters of this religion. The temple's gardens are among the most beautiful in the world.

Brookfield Zoo

Visit the famous zoo in Brookfield. At the zoo you
can watch a porpoise (POR • puss) show. You can see
thousands of different animals. The baboons have
their own hill, called "Baboon Island."

Less than 100 miles northwest of Chicago is the
city of Rockford. Rockford is the second largest city in
Illinois. It is a leader in making machines and

Rock River

machine tools for the rest of the nation. Rockford has
so many trees that it is sometimes called "The
Forest City." You can see that the Rock River has
beautiful scenery.

Peoria (pea • OR • ee • ya) is the third biggest city in
Illinois. Once the Peoria Indians lived here. Today, the
city is a large manufacturing center. Farmers all
over the United States use tractors that were made in
Peoria.

Harvesting soybeans

Out in the country, you see many corn and wheat fields. Some years, Illinois grows more corn than any other state.

Many of those green fields are filled with soybeans. More soybeans are grown in Illinois than in any other state.

Other crops grown in Illinois are barley, rye, alfalfa, apples, asparagus, and melons. Many of these products are bought and sold in Chicago.

In the summer, 300 kinds of birds live in Illinois. But it gets so cold in the winter that most of them fly south.

Fur-bearing animals—skunks, muskrats, opposums, racoons, and rabbits—roam the state. Look hard and you might even see white squirrels.

Many of the towns in Illinois have historical names.

FRENCH NAMES

Joliet (JOE • lee • ett)

Paris (PAIR • iss)

La Salle (LA • SAL)

INDIAN NAMES

Kankakee (kan • kah • KEY)

Peoria (pea • OR • ee • ya)

Ottawa (AW • toh • wah)

Starved Rock

Near La Salle, there is a beautiful place called
Starved Rock. Over two hundred years ago the Illini
(ih • LYE • nye) fought a war with another tribe. The
Illini lost the war. Stories say they were driven to a
high cliff, where they couldn't get food or water.
Many of the Illini starved to death on Starved Rock.

Blacksmith shop in New Salem

New Salem-restored cabin

Covered wagon in New Salem State Park

The Lincoln Statue in New Salem State Park

Illinois is also called the "Land of Lincoln." The 16th president of the United States, Abraham Lincoln, called Illinois his home.

In 1831, long before he became president, Lincoln lived in New Salem (NU SAY • lem), Illinois. Lincoln had many jobs in New Salem. He split rails. He worked in a store. And he worked in the little post office. He was even pilot of a steamboat on the Sangamon (SANG • ah • mawn) River.

New Salem has been rebuilt. The log cabins and stores look just like they did when Lincoln lived there. The steamboat on the river looks just like the one Abraham Lincoln piloted.

State Capitol in Springfield

Eighteen miles southeast of New Salem is Springfield. Springfield is the state capital of Illinois. It was Lincoln's idea to move the capital from Vandalia (van • DAY • lah) to Springfield. He was a state lawmaker then.

In Springfield, you can go inside the house where Lincoln lived. You can see the church the Lincolns went to.

Abraham Lincoln was president of the United States in 1860. When he was president, Lincoln moved to Washington, D.C. But Lincoln loved Illinois, especially Springfield. He is now buried in a large tomb in Springfield.

South of Springfield, there are many mining towns. There is more soft coal in Illinois than in any other state. In Pawnee (paw • knee) one mine produces six million tons of coal each year. It is the biggest mine of its kind in North America.

Cave-in-Rock

Cave-in-Rock

There are 75 state parks in Illinois. Cave-in-Rock State Park is in the southeast tip of the state. The cave goes 108 feet into the bank of the Ohio River. Pirates used to wait in this cave for passing boats. Then they would jump out and rob the people. Years later a gang of outlaws used this cave for a hide-out.

At the southern tip of Illinois the Mississippi and Ohio rivers meet. This land was so rich that the early settlers called it "Little Egypt." There is even a town here called Cairo (KAY • row).

You can go to the Cahokia (ka • HOE • kia) Mounds near East St. Louis, Illinois. There are 40 mounds in the state park. Famous Monk's Mound is 1,037 feet long and 790 feet wide. It is the largest mound in North America.

Grant was head of the Union army during the Civil War. Abraham Lincoln was president at this time.

After the Civil War, General Grant came back to live in Galena. In 1869, he was elected as the 18th president of the United States. When he was done as president, Grant returned to Illinois. You can visit Grant's house in Galena.

Stop at the small town called Union (YOON • yun). Visit the Illinois Railway Museum. Almost every kind of train that ever ran in Illinois is here. There are old steam engines and streetcars. You can even ride some of them.

Chicago with Lake Michigan in background

There is a lot of farm land between Union and Chicago. But soon you see big buildings looming in the distance. Now you are returning to Chicago. You have seen many places in Illinois.

Galena

Illinois is . . . the land of the Mound Builders . . . the land of the Illini Indians . . . the "Land of Lincoln."

The giant city of Chicago . . . hundreds of beautiful towns . . . fields of corn . . . a pirates' cave.

Big and small, there is so much to see in The Prairie State.

Facts About ILLINOIS

Area—56,400 square miles

Highest Point—1,235 (Charles Mound near East Dubuque)

Lowest Point—279 feet (at the delta at Cairo)

Temperature Extremes—High: 117°F (East St. Louis); low: minus 35°F (Mt. Carroll)

Statehood—21st State, December 3, 1818

Counties—102

U.S. Senators—2

U.S. Representatives—24

Capital—Springfield

Other capitals—Kaskaskia (1818-1820) Vandalia (1820-1839)

State Song—"By Thy Rivers Gently Flowing, Illinois," Words by Charles H. Chamberlin new verses by Win Stracke, music by Archibald Johnson

State Slogan—Land of Lincoln

State Motto—*State Sovereignty, National Union*

Familiar Name—Prairie State

Great Seal of Illinois—Authorized March 7, 1867; first used October 26, 1868

State Flag—Designed by Rockford Chapter of D.A.R., became official July 6, 1915

Rivers—Illinois, 273 miles long
   Mississippi, 581 miles (Illinois boundary)
   Ohio, 113 miles (Illinois boundary)

Origin of Name—Some Indians in the region called themselves the *Illini* or *Illiniwek,* meaning *the men;* the word *Illinois* came from the way French settlers pronounced *Illiniwek*

State Flower—Violet
State Bird—Cardinal
State Animal—White-tailed deer
State Insect—Monarch butterfly
State Mineral—Fluorite
State Tree—White oak

Manufacturing Industries—Machinery
(non electric), electrical machinery, fabricated
metal products, food and related products,
primary metals, printing and publishing,
chemicals, transportation equipment,
apparel

Minerals—Coal (bituminous), crude oil, limestone
and dolomite, clay products, portland cement.

Metals -- iron and steel

Agricultural Products—Corn, soybeans, apples,
hogs, cattle

Persons Per Square Mile

100	▇	5,500
50	▢	100
10	▨	50

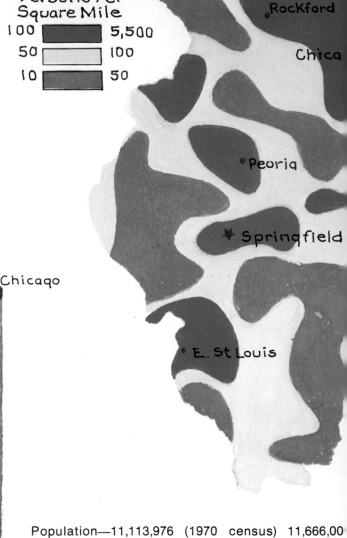

Lead
Zinc
Stone
Sand and Gravel
Chicago
Coal
Coal
Coal
SPRINGFIELD
Stone
Clay
Natural Gas
Oil
Oil
Coal
Oil
Oil
Coal
Fluorite

44

Population—11,113,976 (1970 census) 11,666,00
(1975 estimate)

Population Density—197 persons per square mil

Major Cities—Chicago, (city only) 3,369,35
(1970 census)

Rockford,	147,37
Peoria,	126,96
Springfield,	91,75
East St. Louis,	69,99
Evanston,	80,11
Decatur,	90,39
Cicero,	67,05
Skokie,	68,91
Joliet,	78,88
Aurora,	74,18
Oak Park,	62,51

Illinois History

1673—Jacques Marquette and Louis Joliet come to Illinois.
1680—La Salle builds fort near Peoria.
1699—Cahokia is settled by French.
1703—Kaskaskia settled by French.
1717—Illinois is part of the French Louisiana colony.
1763—French give Illinois to England; French and Indian War ends.
1775—Revolutionary War begins.
1778—George Rogers Clark takes Kaskaskia and Cahokia.
1779—Jean Baptiste Point du Sable builds a trading post at Chicago.
1783—Revolutionary War ends.
1787—Illinois part of the Northwest Territory.
1800—Illinois part of Indiana Territory.
1803—Fort Dearborn built
1809—Kaskaskia capital of Illinois Territory.
1812—Fort Dearborn settlers killed by Indians.
1813—Peoria settled.
1815—Alton settled.
1816—Fort Armstrong begun at Rock Island.
1818—Illinois becomes a state, Dec. 3
1820—Capital moved from Kaskaskia to Vandalia.
1822—Quincy and Urbana settled.
1829—Decatur settled.
1831—Joliet settled.
1832—Black Hawk War (Indians defeated).
1833—Chicago is organized as a town.
1834—Aurora settled.
1835—Waukegan begins; Elgin settled.
1837—Springfield becomes the capital;
      Cairo settled.
1838—First railroad runs in Illinois.
1839—Nauvoo settled.
1843—Bloomington settled; Elmhurst settled.
1848—New state constitution.
1853—First State Fair.
1854—Evanston founded.
1855—Kankakee begun.
1860—Lincoln elected President of the United States.
1861—Civil War begins; East St. Louis incorporated.
1864—President Lincoln reelected; Grant leads
      Union armies.

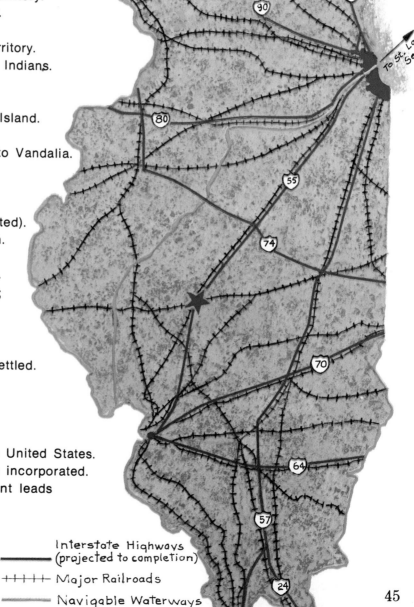

Interstate Highways
(projected to completion)
Major Railroads
Navigable Waterways

45

1865—War ends; Lincoln shot.
1869—Grant becomes President.
1871—Chicago Fire.
1876—State Capitol begun.
1889—Jane Addams opens Hull House.
1892—Granite City established.
1893—World's Columbian Exposition opens in Chicago.
1897—Chicago Loop created by new "L" lines.
1899—Dowie establishes Zion.
1906—New Salem restoration begins.
1913—Women's suffrage law passed by General Assembly.
1917—World War I begins.
1921—Cahokia Mounds scientifically studied for first time.
1937—Oil discovered in Marion County.
1942—1st atomic chain reaction at University of Chicago.
1959—Chicago becomes deep-water port (St. Lawrence Seaway).
1960—Dresden Nuclear Power Plant opens.
1967—Weston gets nuclear accelerator.
1968—Illinois celebrates 150th anniversary of statehood.
1970—Voters approve new state constitution.
1971—Batavia gets world's largest atom smasher.
1973—Sears Tower (the world's tallest building) is completed.
1977—James R. Thompson elected governor.
1980—Illinois schoolchildren choose the white-tailed deer as the
         state animal

INDEX

About the Author:

Dennis Fradin attended Northwestern University on a creative writing scholarship and graduated in 1967. While still at Northwestern, he published his first stories in *Ingenue* magazine and also won a prize in *Seventeen's* short story competition. A prolific writer, Dennis Fradin has been regularly publishing stories in such diverse places as *The Saturday Evening Post, Scholastic, National Humane Review, Midwest,* and *The Teaching Paper.* He has also scripted several educational films. Since 1970 he has taught second grade reading in a Chicago school—a rewarding job, which, the author says, "provides a captive audience on whom I test my children's stories." Married and the father of two children, Dennis Fradin spends his free time with his family or playing a myriad of sports and games with his childhood chums.

About the Artist:

Robert Ulm, a Chicago resident, has been an advertising and editorial artist in both New York and Chicago. Mr. Ulm is a successful painter as well as an illustrator. In his spare time he enjoys fishing and playing tennis.